MUSHROOM CULTIVATION FOR BEGINNERS

The Expert's Guide to Home Mushroom Cultivation. Gourmet and Medicinal Varieties for Indoor and Outdoor Gardeners.

Luis J. Simpson

©2024 by Luis J. Simpson

Mushroom Cultivation For Beginners 2024

TABLE OF CONTENT

Introduction — **6**

CHAPTER ONE — **11**

Understanding Mycology — **11**

The Science of Mushrooms — 11

Benefits of Growing Mushrooms — 14

Overview of Mushroom Varieties — 17

CHAPTER TWO — **20**

Getting Started with Mushroom Cultivation — **20**

Essential Tools and Equipment — 20

Selecting Your Mushroom Species — 23

Creating the Perfect Environment — 26

CHAPTER THREE — **29**

Basic Techniques for Beginners — **29**

Sterilization and Sanitation — 29

Substrate Preparation and Inoculation — 32

Incubation and Colonization — 37

Advanced Cultivation Techniques — **40**

Mastering Grain Spawn Production — 40

Working with Liquid Cultures — 42

Cloning and Tissue Culture — 45

CHAPTER FOUR — **47**

Indoor Mushroom Gardening — **47**

Setting Up an Indoor Grow Room   47

Controlling Temperature and Humidity   50

Lighting and Fresh Air Exchange   52

Outdoor Mushroom Gardening   **54**

Choosing the Right Location   54

Outdoor Beds and Log Cultivation   56

Companion Planting and Permaculture   59

CHAPTER FOUR   **62**

Harvesting and Storage   **62**

When and How to Harvest Mushrooms   62

Drying and Preserving Mushrooms   64

Harvesting Mushrooms for Optimal Freshness 64

Drying Mushrooms for Long-Term Preservation 64

Air Drying   64

Oven Drying   65

Dehydrator Drying   65

Practical Tips and Troubleshooting   65

Preserving Dried Mushrooms: Methods and Best Practices   66

Vacuum-Sealing   67

Freezing   67

Airtight Containers   67

Labeling and Organizing   68

Optimal Shelf Life   68

Troubleshooting Common Issues   **72**

Identifying Contamination   72

Pest and Disease Management   75

Solving Environmental Challenges   80

CHAPTER FIVE 83

Exploring Gourmet and Medicinal Varieties 83

Popular Gourmet Mushrooms 83

Medicinal Mushrooms and Their Uses 86

Medicinal Mushrooms and Their Uses 89

Crafting Nature's Cure – The Medicinal Magic of
Mushrooms 92

Introduction

Embark on an extraordinary journey into the enchanting realm of mushroom cultivation, where the mysteries of mycology unfold in the comfort of your own home. This book is your comprehensive guide to nurturing a diverse array of gourmet and medicinal mushrooms, a testament to nature's generosity and complexity. Whether you're a novice gardener seeking to cultivate your first Shiitake or a seasoned mycophile dreaming of a lush Lion's

Mane harvest, these pages will illuminate the path with expert knowledge and passionate guidance.

Discover the art and science that transforms spores into culinary treasures and healing wonders. With each chapter, you'll delve deeper into the fascinating lifecycle of fungi, learning how to create the perfect environment for indoor and outdoor growth. From the rich, earthy aroma of Porcini to the delicate caps of Enoki, the world of mushrooms offers an endless palette of flavors and health benefits.

As you turn these pages, prepare to be captivated by the potential that lies in a single spore. The journey ahead is not just about growing mushrooms—it's about cultivating a deeper connection with the natural world and unlocking the full potential of these remarkable organisms. Welcome to the transformative experience of mushroom cultivation, where every gardener can find joy and wonder in the simple act of watching mushrooms grow.

White Button
Cremini (Baby Bella)
Portobello
Shiitake
Oyster

Maitake (Hen of the Woods)
Porcini
Chanterelle
Enoki
Morel

Lion's Mane
Wood Ear
Black
Trumpet
King Trumpet
Beech

CHAPTER ONE

Understanding Mycology

The Science of Mushrooms

In the fascinating chapter of "Understanding Mycology: The Science of Mushrooms," we immerse ourselves in the intricate world of fungi, a kingdom of life that remains largely enigmatic and profoundly influential. This chapter is dedicated to unraveling the complexities of mycology, making the science behind mushrooms accessible and engaging to all readers.

The Fungal Foundation

Mycology is the scientific study of fungi, a group of organisms that are critical to the health of our planet. Fungi are not plants; they belong to their own kingdom, distinct in their cellular structure and life cycle. In this section, we explore the basic biology of fungi, from their cell walls made of chitin to their unique reproductive strategies involving spores.

Spores: The Seeds of the Fungal World

Spores are to fungi what seeds are to plants. These microscopic particles are the starting point for the fungal life cycle. We'll delve into the conditions that trigger spore release and the factors that influence their germination and growth into mycelium, the vegetative part of a fungus.

The Mycelial Web

The mycelium is the true powerhouse of a fungus, a vast and intricate network of hyphae that can span acres. It's the mycelium that forges symbiotic relationships with plants, decomposes organic matter, and ultimately gives rise to the mushrooms we see and eat.

Mushrooms: The Fruiting Bodies

Mushrooms are the fruiting bodies of fungi, the reproductive structures that emerge from the mycelium. They come in an astonishing variety of shapes, sizes, and colors, each adapted to its environment and role in the ecosystem.

Symbiosis: Fungi and Plants in Harmony

Many fungi form symbiotic relationships with plants, known as mycorrhizae. These partnerships are vital for the health of our forests and crops. Fungi help plants absorb water and nutrients, while plants provide the fungi with sugars produced through photosynthesis.

Fungi as Decomposers and Recyclers

Fungi play a crucial role as decomposers, breaking down dead organic material and recycling it back into the ecosystem. Without fungi, our world would be buried in waste.

Cultivating Mushrooms

Mushroom cultivation is both a science and an art. In this section, we guide readers through the process of growing mushrooms at home, from selecting the right substrate to creating the ideal conditions for fruiting.

Challenges and Rewards of Home Cultivation

Growing mushrooms at home can be challenging, but it's also incredibly rewarding. We'll share stories of success and failure, providing tips and tricks to help readers overcome common obstacles.

The Medicinal Power of Mushrooms

Mushrooms are not just food; they have been used for their medicinal properties for thousands of years. We'll explore the science behind these claims, examining how compounds found in mushrooms can support our health.

Benefits of Growing Mushrooms

Imagine transforming a small corner of your home into a lush, miniature forest where gourmet mushrooms bloom like woodland treasures. This is the delightful reality of home mushroom cultivation, a hobby that brings the wonders of the natural world right to your kitchen and offers a bounty of benefits.

Culinary Delights Right at Your Fingertips Growing your own mushrooms means you have access to a variety of fresh, gourmet options that can elevate any meal. From the meaty texture of Portobellos to the delicate flavor of Enokis, home cultivation allows you to experiment with species that may not be readily available or affordable at your local market. Imagine the satisfaction of adding home-grown Shiitake mushrooms to your stir-fry or topping your pizza with a generous helping of Chanterelles, harvested right from your own mushroom patch.

Sustainability in Every Spore Mushroom cultivation is a sustainable practice that can reduce your carbon footprint. Mushrooms require minimal space and resources to grow, making them an ideal crop for urban gardeners. They can be grown on a variety of substrates, often utilizing waste products like coffee grounds, sawdust, or straw. This not only recycles what would otherwise be trash but also produces nutritious food, embodying the principles of a circular economy.

An Eco-Friendly Endeavor By growing mushrooms, you're contributing to environmental health. Mushrooms play a vital role in our ecosystems by breaking down organic matter and returning nutrients to the soil. By cultivating them, you're participating in this natural process and fostering a more sustainable relationship with our planet.

Anecdotes of Mushroom Mastery Consider the story of Ruth, a city dweller with no prior gardening experience, who started growing oyster mushrooms in a small container in her apartment. Within weeks, she was harvesting her own mushrooms, adding them to pastas, salads, and omelets, and sharing the surplus with her neighbors. Or take the example of retired engineer Raj, who turned his fascination with fungi into a thriving backyard operation, finding joy in the daily care of his mushroom beds and the community that formed around his abundant harvests.

Personal Satisfaction and Well-Being Beyond the tangible benefits, growing mushrooms can be a deeply fulfilling experience. It's a meditative process that requires patience and attention, offering a welcome respite from the hustle and bustle of daily life. The act of nurturing something from spore to fruit can be a source of personal satisfaction and well-being.

Overview of Mushroom Varieties

Let's take a stroll through the enchanting forest of mushroom varieties, each with its own story and a special place in the kitchen or medicine cabinet. Imagine you're walking through a bustling farmers' market, and with each step, you discover a new mushroom friend.

Button Mushrooms: These are the friendly neighbors you see all the time. They're versatile and mild, perfect for any dish that needs a subtle, earthy touch. Saute them, grill them, or toss them in a salad—they're always ready to please.

Portobello Mushrooms: The gentle giants of the mushroom world. With their large caps and meaty texture, they're ideal for grilling and stuffing. They make a hearty substitute for meat in burgers, giving you that satisfying bite with a smoky flavor.

Shiitake Mushrooms: These mushrooms have a rich, smoky flavor that deepens any stir-fry or soup. They're also revered for their medicinal properties, believed to support the immune system. Cultivating shiitake at home can be a rewarding experience, both for your taste buds and your health.

Oyster Mushrooms: Delicate and tender, with a hint of sweetness, oyster mushrooms are like the fluttering butterflies of the forest. They grow in beautiful clusters and can add elegance to any dish. Plus, they're known for their cholesterol-lowering abilities.

Enoki Mushrooms: Tall, slender, and with a crisp texture, enokis are the ballerinas of mushrooms. They dance wonderfully in soups and salads, offering a crunchy contrast to softer ingredients.

Morel Mushrooms: These are the hidden treasures, highly sought after for their nutty and earthy flavor. They're like the truffles of the mushroom family, turning any dish into a gourmet experience.

Reishi Mushrooms: Often found in wellness teas and supplements, reishi is the wise old sage of mushrooms. It's not typically used in cooking due to its bitter taste, but its potential benefits for boosting the immune system and reducing stress make it a valuable addition to your home apothecary.

Lion's Mane: With a look as unique as its name, lion's mane mushrooms have a seafood-like flavor, often compared to crab or lobster. They're not just a culinary delight; they're also studied for their nerve-regenerative properties.

CHAPTER TWO

Getting Started with Mushroom Cultivation

Essential Tools and Equipment

 Having the right tools and equipment will set you up for success. Let's explore the essentials that will help you grow beautiful, bountiful mushrooms.

1. Spawn Jars or Bags

Purpose: These are containers for your mushroom spawn, the material inoculated with mushroom mycelium. Think of them as the cozy nurseries where your mushrooms begin their life.

Use: You'll fill these with a nutrient-rich substrate, inoculate them with spawn, and watch as the mycelium weaves its magic, turning the substrate into a network of potential mushrooms.

2. Pressure Cooker or Autoclave

Purpose: Sterilization is key in mushroom cultivation to prevent contamination. A pressure cooker or autoclave is used to sterilize your substrates and tools.

Use: Like a superhero zapping villains, this tool will eliminate unwanted bacteria and fungi, ensuring a clean start for your mushrooms.

3. Substrate

Purpose: This is the food for your mushrooms. Substrates can be made from various materials like straw, wood chips, or grain, depending on the mushroom species.

Use: You'll mix, pasteurize or sterilize, and then inoculate your substrate, creating a banquet for your mushrooms to feast on.

4. Inoculation Loop or Needle

Purpose: This tool is used for transferring mushroom spores or mycelium to your substrate without contamination.

Use: With a steady hand, you'll feel like a scientist as you carefully introduce the essence of life to your substrate.

5. Hygrometer and Thermometer

Purpose: Mushrooms need specific humidity and temperature ranges to thrive. These instruments measure and help you monitor these conditions.

Use: Keep an eye on these, and you'll become the guardian of the perfect mushroom-growing climate.

6. Spray Bottle or Misting System

Purpose: Moisture is crucial for mushrooms. A spray bottle or misting system helps maintain the necessary humidity.

Use: Gently misting your mushrooms, you'll create rain showers in their micro-environment, vital for their growth.

7. Grow Tent or Grow Box

Purpose: This provides a controlled environment for your mushrooms to grow, free from outside contaminants and with stable conditions.

Use: Inside this space, you'll create a mini-universe tailored just for your mushrooms, where they can safely expand and flourish.

8. Gloves and Masks

Purpose: Personal protective equipment keeps both you and your mushrooms safe from contaminants.

Use: Suit up with these, and you'll be the protector of purity in your mushroom domain.

As you gather these tools, imagine the journey you're about to take. Each item is a key to unlocking the potential of your mushroom crop. With these in hand, you're not just growing mushrooms; you're cultivating a new skill, nurturing life, and perhaps even finding a new passion.

Selecting Your Mushroom Species

Embarking on your mushroom cultivation journey is like stepping into a forest of possibilities. The key to a rewarding experience lies in choosing the right mushroom species that align with your skill level, environment, and what you hope to achieve. Let's walk through the forest together and find the perfect mushroom companions for you.

Understanding Mushroom Varieties

Mushrooms come in all shapes, sizes, and flavors. Some are perfect for the culinary adventurer, while others boast medicinal properties that have been cherished for centuries. To start, familiarize yourself with two broad categories:

- **Gourmet Mushrooms**: These include varieties like **Oyster, Shiitake**, and **Portobello**. They are known for their delicious taste and are a great starting point for those looking to add home-grown flavor to their meals.
- **Medicinal Mushrooms**: Species like **Reishi, Lion's Mane**, and **Turkey Tail** are sought after for their health benefits, ranging from immune support to cognitive enhancement.

Consider Your Growing Space

Where you plan to grow your mushrooms will significantly influence your choice. Ask yourself:

- Do I have space indoors for a small grow tent or shelf?
- Is there a shady spot in my garden that could become a mushroom haven?

Match Your Skill Level

Some mushrooms are more forgiving than others. As a beginner, look for species that are:

- **Resilient**: Oyster mushrooms are hardy and can grow in various substrates, making them ideal for beginners.
- **Fast-Growing**: Species like the **White Button mushroom** mature quickly, offering a gratifying harvest in a short time.

Think About Your Goals

Are you growing mushrooms for their taste, health benefits, or both? Your goals will guide your selection:

- For culinary delight, start with **Oyster** or **Shiitake** mushrooms.
- If wellness is your aim, try cultivating **Reishi** or **Lion's Mane**.

Practical Tips for Selection

1. **Start Small**: Choose one or two species to begin with. This will help you focus and learn without feeling overwhelmed.
2. **Research**: Read about the mushrooms you're interested in. Understand their needs and how they fit into your life.
3. **Source Quality Spores**: Obtain spores or spawn from reputable suppliers to ensure a healthy start for your mushrooms.

Embrace the Adventure

Selecting your mushroom species is the first step in a journey of growth and discovery. Each mushroom has its personality, and as you learn to cultivate them, you'll also learn about the rhythms of nature and the joy of nurturing life. So take a deep breath, choose your mushrooms with confidence, and get ready to watch them thrive under your care.

Remember, every cultivator starts as a beginner, and every expert was once where you are now. With patience and curiosity, you'll not only grow mushrooms but also cultivate a new sense of connection with the natural world.

Creating the Perfect Environment

Imagine you're a wizard in the enchanted forest, tasked with the noble quest of cultivating the most magical of all ingredients: mushrooms. Your mission is to create a sanctuary where these delicate treasures can flourish. Here's how you can conjure the perfect environment for your mushroom companions.

Temperature: Mushrooms are like Goldilocks; they prefer conditions that are not too hot, not too cold, but just right. Most varieties thrive in a gentle **60-75°F** (15-24°C). Think of it as the cozy warmth of a spring morning, where the air is fresh but the chill of winter is a distant memory.

Humidity: Mushrooms bask in moisture like morning dew on a spider's web. They need a humidity level of about **80-95%**. To achieve this, you might use a misting spell to shower them lightly throughout the day, ensuring they're never parched nor drowned.

Lighting: While mushrooms don't rely on sunlight like plants, they do enjoy a soft glow, akin to the dappled light that filters through the leaves. A few hours of indirect light will guide them on their growth journey, just enough to whisper the tales of the world above.

Now, let's bring our story to life with a practical example. Imagine you've found a spot in your home, perhaps a closet or a corner, where you can set up a small mushroom grove. You install a **thermostat** to keep the temperature steady, a **humidifier** to mimic the forest's breath, and a

shade cloth to soften the light from a nearby window.

As days pass, you watch in awe as tiny pins emerge from the soil, growing into proud caps and stems. With each new mushroom, your confidence blooms, and the excitement of harvest fills the air. You've not only created the perfect environment for mushrooms, but you've also nurtured a piece of the enchanted forest in your own realm.

CHAPTER THREE

Basic Techniques for Beginners

Sterilization and Sanitation

Sterilization and sanitation are the unsung heroes of mushroom cultivation. Think of them as the invisible shields that protect your mushroom kingdom from the unseen enemies – bacteria, molds, and yeasts that can spoil your crop.

Why Sterilization and Sanitation Matter In the world of mushrooms, cleanliness isn't just next to godliness; it's essential for survival. Mushrooms are delicate organisms that thrive in specific conditions, but so do many contaminants. If you're not careful, these unwanted guests will crash your mushroom party and take over, leaving you with nothing but a mess.

Sterilization: The Heat is On Sterilization is like sending your substrate (the material on which mushrooms grow) through a boot camp. You're training it to resist invaders by exposing it to high heat. This can be done through methods like steam sterilization or using a pressure cooker. Imagine you're preparing a fortress for your mushroom spores – you want to make sure no other microbe can breach its walls.

Sanitation: Cleanliness is Key Sanitation is the daily practice of keeping things clean. It's washing your hands before handling materials, wiping down surfaces with alcohol, and wearing gloves and a mask. Think of it as the daily drills to keep your mushroom troops in top shape, ready to fend off any microbial attack.

Step-by-Step Guide to Sterilization and Sanitation

1. **Prepare Your Substrate**: Choose a substrate that suits your mushroom variety. Common choices are grains, straw, or wood chips.
2. **Sterilize Your Substrate**: If using a pressure cooker, fill it with a few inches of water, place your substrate-filled jars or bags inside, and heat at 15 PSI for 60-90 minutes. No pressure cooker? No problem. You can

pasteurize your substrate by soaking it in hot water at 65-80°C for an hour.

3. **Sanitize Your Workspace**: Wipe down all surfaces with a 10% bleach solution or 70% isopropyl alcohol. This is like setting up a force field around your cultivation area.

4. **Inoculate with Care**: After cooling the substrate, introduce your mushroom spores or mycelium in a clean environment. This could be a still-air box or a laminar flow hood if you're feeling fancy.

5. **Incubate with Patience**: Store your inoculated substrate in a clean, controlled environment. Keep an eye out for any signs of contamination – they usually show up as colorful patches that aren't mushroom mycelium.

6. **Fruit with Joy**: Once fully colonized, expose your substrate to fresh air and the right humidity for mushrooms to fruit. Keep everything clean to avoid late-stage contamination.

Common Pitfalls and Best Practices

- **Avoid Cross-Contamination**: Always work with one culture at a time to prevent cross-contamination.

- **Be Patient**: Rushing can lead to mistakes. Take your time with each step.
- **Monitor Your Crops**: Keep an eye out for any unusual growths or colors, and remove contaminated substrates immediately.

Substrate Preparation and Inoculation

Substrate preparation and inoculation are the foundational steps that set the stage for a bountiful harvest. Let's walk through these steps together, as if I'm right there in your garden, sharing a cup of tea and some friendly advice on nurturing your very own fungal friends.

Substrate Preparation: Your Mushroom's Home Sweet Home

Choose Your Base: Think of the substrate as the soil for your mushrooms. It's their home, and you want to make it as cozy as possible. Common choices include straw, hardwood sawdust, or coffee grounds. Each mushroom species has its preference, so pick the substrate that's best suited for your chosen variety.

Size Matters: Break down your substrate into small pieces. This increases the surface area and makes it easier for the mushroom mycelium to colonize. Imagine you're preparing a fluffy bed for the mycelium to snuggle into.

Moisture is Key: Your substrate needs to be moist, but not wet. Aim for the consistency of a well-wrung sponge. If you squeeze a handful and only a few drops of water come out, you've hit the sweet spot.

Sterilize to Sanitize: Now, it's time to get rid of any unwanted microbes. You can steam your substrate or bake it in an oven. If you're using a pressure cooker, 15 PSI for 90 minutes should do the trick. It's like giving your substrate a spa day to ensure it's clean and ready for the mycelium to move in.

Inoculation: Welcoming the Mycelium to Its New Home

Clean and Serene: Before you start, clean your workspace and tools. Wear gloves and a mask to keep things sterile. It's like preparing a nursery for a newborn – everything needs to be spotless.

Introduce the Mycelium: Using a syringe or a spawn jar, introduce the mycelium to the substrate.

Be gentle and quick. It's a bit like planting seeds in a garden; you want to do it with care and love.

Seal the Deal: Once the mycelium is in, seal your bags or jars to protect them from contaminants. But remember, the mycelium needs to breathe, so use a filter patch or leave a small opening for air exchange.

Patience is a Virtue: Store your inoculated substrate in a dark, warm place and wait for the mycelium to colonize it. This can take a few weeks, so be patient. It's like waiting for dough to rise – it takes time, but the results are worth it.

Common Mistakes to Avoid

Over-moistening the Substrate: Too much water can drown your mycelium. Aim for damp, not soggy.

Skipping Sterilization: This step is crucial. Without it, you're rolling out the red carpet for contaminants.

Rushing the Inoculation: Take your time. A rushed job can lead to mistakes and contamination.Substrate preparation and inoculation are the foundational steps that set the stage for a bountiful harvest. Let's walk through these steps together, as if I'm right there in your garden, sharing a cup of tea and some friendly advice on nurturing your very own fungal friends.

Substrate Preparation: Your Mushroom's Home Sweet Home

1. **Choose Your Base**: Think of the substrate as the soil for your mushrooms. It's their home, and you want to make it as cozy as possible. Common choices include **straw, hardwood sawdust, or coffee grounds**. Each mushroom species has its preference, so pick the substrate that's best suited for your chosen variety.
2. **Size Matters**: Break down your substrate into small pieces. This increases the surface area and makes it easier for the mushroom mycelium to colonize. Imagine you're preparing a fluffy bed for the mycelium to snuggle into.
3. **Moisture is Key**: Your substrate needs to be moist, but not wet. Aim for the consistency of a well-wrung sponge. If you squeeze a handful and only a few drops of water come out, you've hit the sweet spot.
4. **Sterilize to Sanitize**: Now, it's time to get rid of any unwanted microbes. You can steam your substrate or bake it in an oven. If you're using a pressure cooker, 15 PSI for 90 minutes should do the trick. It's like giving your substrate a spa day to ensure it's clean and ready for the mycelium to move in.

Inoculation: Welcoming the Mycelium to Its New Home

1. **Clean and Serene**: Before you start, clean your workspace and tools. Wear gloves and a mask to keep things sterile. It's like preparing a nursery for a newborn – everything needs to be spotless.
2. **Introduce the Mycelium**: Using a syringe or a spawn jar, introduce the mycelium to the substrate. Be gentle and quick. It's a bit like planting seeds in a garden; you want to do it with care and love.
3. **Seal the Deal**: Once the mycelium is in, seal your bags or jars to protect them from contaminants. But remember, the mycelium needs to breathe, so use a filter patch or leave a small opening for air exchange.
4. **Patience is a Virtue**: Store your inoculated substrate in a dark, warm place and wait for the mycelium to colonize it. This can take a few weeks, so be patient. It's like waiting for dough to rise – it takes time, but the results are worth it.

Common Mistakes to Avoid

- **Over-moistening the Substrate**: Too much water can drown your mycelium. Aim for damp, not soggy.
- **Skipping Sterilization**: This step is crucial. Without it, you're rolling out the red carpet for contaminants.
- **Rushing the Inoculation**: Take your time. A rushed job can lead to mistakes and contamination.

Incubation and Colonization

Imagine you've just tucked your little mushroom spores into their beds, all snug within the substrate. Now comes the part where you, as a mushroom cultivator, play the waiting game, but it's also where the magic happens: **Incubation and Colonization**.

Incubation: The Cozy Nap Time for Spores

Incubation is like the hibernation phase for your mushrooms. You've introduced the spores or mycelium to the substrate, and now they need a quiet, undisturbed place to grow. This is their time

to stretch out, yawn, and slowly wake up to their
new world.

- **Temperature**: Keep it just right. Not too
  hot, not too cold. For most mushrooms, this
  means a cozy **70-75°F (21-24°C)**.
- **Darkness**: Mushrooms don't need light at
  this stage. A dark cupboard or a corner of a
  room works perfectly. It's like providing a
  dark, comfortable room for a good night's
  sleep.
- **Humidity**: Keep the air around them moist.
  You want to mimic the feeling of a misty
  morning in a lush forest.

Colonization: The Mycelium Takes Over

As the mycelium wakes up, it starts to colonize the
substrate. This is where it spreads its tiny,
thread-like cells throughout its new home, creating
a white, web-like network. It's like watching a
plant's roots grow in fast-forward.

- **Patience is Key**: This part takes time.
  Depending on the mushroom, it can be
  anywhere from a week to a month. It's like
  waiting for bread to rise; you can't rush it.
- **Look, Don't Touch**: Resist the urge to
  poke around. The mycelium is delicate and

doesn't like to be disturbed. It's like baking a cake – keep the oven door closed!

Why This Matters

Incubation and colonization are critical because they set the stage for healthy mushroom growth. If the mycelium doesn't colonize well, your mushrooms won't grow well. It's like laying the foundation for a house; it needs to be strong and well-built.

Relatable Example

Think of it like planting a garden. You've put the seeds in the soil (inoculation), and now you're waiting for them to sprout and spread their roots (colonization). You wouldn't dig up the seeds every day to check on them, right? The same goes for mushrooms. Give them time and space, and they'll do their thing.

Simple Language Tip

If you're ever unsure if your mushrooms are colonizing correctly, look for a white, fluffy substance spreading throughout the substrate. That's your mycelium, and it's a good sign!

Advanced Cultivation Techniques

Mastering Grain Spawn Production

Embarking on the journey of mushroom cultivation can be as enchanting as entering a forest filled with hidden treasures. Mastering grain spawn production is a pivotal step in this adventure, and I'm here to guide you through it with clarity and ease.

Step 1: Choosing Your Grain Begin with selecting your base; grains such as rye, wheat, or millet serve as excellent substrates. They are the 'soil' where your mushroom 'seeds' will flourish. Opt for organic grains to ensure the healthiest start for your mushrooms.

Step 2: Preparing the Grain Hydration is key. Soak your grains in water for 12-24 hours to awaken them from their slumber. After soaking, simmer them until they are plump with moisture, yet firm to the touch. This balance is crucial; too much water and your grains will become a breeding ground for bacteria, too little and your mushrooms will thirst for nutrients.

Step 3: Sterilization Sterility is the guardian of your grain spawn. Pack your hydrated grains into jars and seal them with a breathable filter. Autoclave or pressure cook them to banish unwanted microorganisms. This step is your shield against contamination.

Step 4: Inoculation In a clean environment, introduce your mushroom spores or mycelium to the sterilized grain. This is the spark of life, the beginning of your mushroom's journey. Be swift and careful; this is a delicate dance with nature.

Step 5: Incubation Place your inoculated jars in a warm, dark place. Like a caterpillar in a cocoon, the mycelium will weave its web throughout the grain. This is the waiting game, where patience is rewarded with growth.

Step 6: Observation and Care Monitor your jars for signs of life. White, fluffy mycelium should spread like morning frost across a windowpane. If you spot any colors of mold, it's a sign to adjust your process. Learn from these encounters; they are the teachers of the forest.

Step 7: Expansion or Fruiting Once fully colonized, your grain spawn is ready to conquer new lands. You can either expand it by adding more grain or introduce it to a fruiting substrate like straw or wood chips. This is where your mushrooms will come into their own, reaching for the sky.

Remember, every mushroom cultivator was once a beginner, standing at the edge of the forest, curious and eager. With each batch of grain spawn, you'll gain wisdom and skill. Embrace the process, for it's not just about growing mushrooms, but also about growing yourself as a cultivator.

Working with Liquid Cultures

Imagine embarking on a journey where you become an alchemist of sorts, transforming a simple liquid into a thriving culture teeming with potential. This is the art of working with liquid cultures in mushroom cultivation, a technique that can seem like magic to the uninitiated but is grounded in science and patience. Let's dive into this fascinating process together.

Step 1: Understanding Liquid Cultures Liquid cultures are a suspension of mushroom mycelium in a nutrient-rich liquid solution. Think of it as a concentrated life force of your future mushrooms, ready to spring into action. It's a way to propagate your fungi faster and more efficiently than traditional spore syringes.

Step 2: Gathering Your Materials You'll need a few key items:

- A **sterile syringe** to extract and inject the culture.
- **Mason jars** or similar containers for storing the culture.
- A **pressure cooker** for sterilization.
- A **nutrient broth** made from water, honey, or malt extract to feed your mycelium.

Step 3: Preparing the Nutrient Broth Combine water with a small amount of honey or malt extract. This sweet concoction will be the food that fuels your mycelium's growth. Sterilize the solution by boiling or pressure cooking it to create a safe environment for your culture.

Step 4: Inoculation In a clean, sterile environment, introduce mushroom spores or a piece of mycelium into the cooled nutrient broth. This is where the magic begins. The mycelium will start to consume the nutrients and multiply.

Step 5: Incubation Store your inoculated jars in a dark, warm place. Over the next days to weeks, you'll witness a transformation as the mycelium colonizes the liquid. It's a living network, expanding its reach like branches of a tree.

Step 6: Expansion Once your liquid culture is teeming with mycelium, it's ready to be used. With a sterile syringe, you can extract the culture and inject it into grain jars or bags to further expand your mycelium or directly into your fruiting substrate.

Step 7: Fruiting After transferring your mycelium into its new home, provide the right conditions for fruiting. With patience and care, you'll soon see the fruits of your labor – actual mushrooms!

Remember, working with liquid cultures is like nurturing a garden. It requires attention, cleanliness, and a bit of wonder at the natural processes at work. As you gain experience, you'll develop a deeper connection with the life cycle of mushrooms and a greater appreciation for the delicate balance of cultivation.

So, don your alchemist's hat, and let's turn this liquid gold into bountiful harvests. With each step, feel the excitement of unlocking the secrets of mushroom cultivation and the empowerment that comes with mastering this advanced technique.

Cloning and Tissue Culture

Imagine you're a gardener, but instead of growing plants from seeds, you're creating identical copies of your favorite mushroom. That's **cloning** in a nutshell. It's like taking a cutting from a plant, but for mushrooms, you take a piece of the fungus itself and encourage it to grow into a new one. This is great because you know exactly what kind of mushroom you'll get since it's a carbon copy of the parent.

Now, let's talk about **tissue culture**. Think of it as a high-tech nursery for your mushrooms. You take a tiny piece of the mushroom, even just a few cells, and place it in a special nutrient-rich jelly called agar. It's like giving the cells a comfy bed and all the food they need to grow. Under the right conditions, these cells will multiply and eventually form a whole new mushroom. It's a bit like baking a cake with a recipe – if you follow the steps and give it time, you'll end up with something delicious.

Both cloning and tissue culture are ways to get more of the mushrooms you love, but they also have bigger benefits. They can help save space, reduce waste, and even help with research on how to make mushrooms healthier and more resistant to diseases.

CHAPTER FOUR

Indoor Mushroom Gardening

Setting Up an Indoor Grow Room

Embarking on the adventure of growing mushrooms indoors can be both exciting and a bit daunting. But fear not! I'm here to guide you through each step, ensuring you feel supported and confident as you create a little haven for your fungi friends. Let's get started!

Step 1: Choosing Your Space

Find a space in your home that you can dedicate to your mushrooms. It doesn't have to be large—a closet, a corner of your basement, or a spare room will do. The key is consistency in conditions and minimal disturbances.

Step 2: Cleanliness is Key

Before anything else, clean your space thoroughly. Mushrooms are sensitive to contaminants, so disinfect surfaces with a solution of 10% bleach to prevent any unwanted spores from crashing your mushroom party.

Step 3: Setting Up Shelving

Install shelving units to maximize your space. Adjustable shelves are great as they can accommodate different sizes of mushroom containers as your cultivation skills grow.

Step 4: Lighting It Right

Mushrooms don't require much light, but they do need some. Install a few **LED lights** or use natural light if available, but avoid direct sunlight. A simple timer can ensure they receive a consistent light schedule.

Step 5: Maintaining Moisture

Mushrooms love humidity. You can maintain a humid environment by misting the air regularly or using a humidifier. Aim for a humidity level of about 95%, but ensure there's enough ventilation to prevent mold.

Step 6: Air Circulation

Good air exchange is crucial. Set up a small fan to keep the air moving, but make sure it's not pointed directly at your mushrooms to avoid drying them out.

Step 7: Temperature Control

Most mushrooms thrive at temperatures between **55-75°F** (13-24°C). Use a heater or air conditioner to maintain a stable temperature within this range.

Step 8: Starting with Spores

Purchase mushroom spores or spawn from a reputable source. There are many varieties, so start with one that's known to be more forgiving for beginners, like oyster mushrooms.

Step 9: Substrate Preparation

Prepare your substrate (the material your mushrooms will grow on). Common substrates include straw, wood chips, or a soil mixture. Sterilize it to prevent contamination, then inoculate it with your spores or spawn.

Step 10: Patience and Observation

After inoculation, give your mushrooms time to grow. This is a period of waiting and watching. Keep an eye on moisture and temperature, and adjust as needed.

Remember, mushroom cultivation is as much an art as it is a science. Don't be discouraged if your first try isn't perfect.

Controlling Temperature and Humidity

In the serene world of indoor mushroom gardening, the whisper of mist and the gentle warmth of a controlled environment are the silent symphonies that encourage the delicate growth of these fascinating fungi. **Temperature and humidity** are the conductors of this quiet orchestra, orchestrating a balance that is crucial for the thriving of your mushroom garden.

Temperature, the unseen embrace that surrounds your mushrooms, should be maintained with a nurturing touch. Most mushrooms flourish within the **18°C to 24°C** range, a cozy bracket where they can comfortably unfurl their caps. Too cold, and they may slumber in dormancy; too warm, and they might wilt in distress. A reliable thermometer and gentle heating or cooling methods can help you maintain this delicate equilibrium.

Humidity, on the other hand, is the lifeblood of moisture that mushrooms crave. It's a veil of wetness in the air, a cloak that keeps them supple and spry. Aim for a humidity level around **85% to 95%** for most varieties, creating an environment reminiscent of the earth's nurturing embrace. A hygrometer, paired with a humidifier or a simple spray bottle, can be your tools of choice to weave this moist mantle.

Here are some practical tips to help you manage these vital elements:

- **Monitor daily**: Keep a close eye on temperature and humidity with accurate instruments.
- **Automate**: Consider investing in a thermostat and humidistat to automate the regulation.
- **Ventilate**: Ensure good air circulation to distribute heat and moisture evenly.
- **Insulate**: Use insulation to maintain a consistent temperature, especially in cooler climates.
- **Mist**: Regular misting can boost humidity, but avoid over-saturation which can lead to mold.

Remember, each mushroom species may whisper its unique needs, so tailor your care to their individual whispers. With patience and attentiveness, you can create a sanctuary where mushrooms not only grow but thrive, offering you not just a harvest of crops, but a harvest of tranquility and connection to the natural world.

Lighting and Fresh Air Exchange

Creating a successful indoor mushroom garden hinges on two critical factors: lighting and fresh air exchange. Let's delve into how you can optimize these elements for a bountiful harvest.

Lighting

Mushrooms thrive under specific lighting conditions that mimic the natural sunlight they would receive in the wild. Here are some practical tips to optimize lighting for your indoor mushroom garden:

Light Types: LED lights are highly recommended for mushroom cultivation due to their energy efficiency, long lifespan, and low heat emission.

Light Spectrum: Mushrooms generally require blue and red light for optimal growth. Blue light promotes vegetative growth, while red light is essential during the fruiting stage.

Intensity and Duration: Aim for a low to moderate light intensity, between 500 and 2000 lux, and a duration of 8 to 12 hours per day to prevent inhibiting fruiting or causing deformities.

Fresh Air Exchange (FAE)

Proper air circulation is crucial for mushroom development, as it helps to replace the CO2-rich air with fresh, oxygen-rich air. Here's how to ensure effective fresh air exchange:

Monotub Method: Utilize a monotub grow kit with small holes covered with polyfill or micropore tape to facilitate gas exchange without letting in contaminants.

Ventilation System: Incorporate a fresh air exchange fan in your setup to maintain a healthy growing environment. A negative pressure system, which pulls air out of the room, is advisable to keep the environment clean.

Frequency: Generally, mushrooms should be exposed to fresh air at least once every 24 hours. Some species may require more frequent air exchange.

By understanding and implementing these fundamental elements, even beginner cultivators can create thriving indoor mushroom gardens bursting with vitality and flavor.

Outdoor Mushroom Gardening

Choosing the Right Location

outdoor mushroom garden is akin to discovering a hidden treasure in your backyard. It's a process filled with anticipation and delight, where each step brings you closer to the earth and its bountiful gifts.

Finding the Perfect Spot: The quest for the perfect location is the first step. Mushrooms are not like your typical garden plants; they thrive in the gentle embrace of shade rather than the bright caress of the sun. Look for a spot that is **shielded from direct sunlight**, perhaps under the dappled light of a tree or on the north side of a structure. Remember, mushrooms are the understory of nature's grand forest canopy.

Moisture – The Lifeblood of Mushrooms: Mushrooms love moisture; it's the lifeblood that fuels their growth. You'll want to find a spot where the soil retains dampness without becoming waterlogged. Think of the forest floor after a gentle rain, how it holds onto the droplets like precious pearls. That's what your mushrooms will need. A place where the morning dew lingers a bit longer, perhaps near a pond or a stream, can be ideal.

Natural Protection – A Mushroom's Guardian: Just as a fledgling needs the protection of its nest, your mushroom garden requires natural guardians. Overhanging leaves, a fallen log, or even a man-made structure can provide the necessary shelter from the elements. These guardians also offer a microclimate that can help regulate temperature and humidity, key factors in mushroom cultivation.

Envisioning Your Tranquil Garden: Now, close your eyes and picture this tranquil space. It's a corner of your world where time slows down, and nature whispers. You can almost hear the soft rustle of mushroom caps pushing through the leaf litter, reaching for the air. It's a place where every visit feels like you're checking in on an old friend, watching with pride as they grow.

A Personal Touch: In my own experience, there's something magical about tending to a mushroom garden. It's a reminder of nature's cycles and the quiet power of growth. I recall the joy of spotting the first tiny cap peeking out, a sign of success and the promise of many harvests to come.

Outdoor Beds and Log Cultivation

Setting up an outdoor mushroom bed is like creating a little ecosystem for your fungi friends to thrive in. It's a delightful project that connects you with nature and yields delicious results. Let's walk through the steps together, shall we?

Selecting the Right Location: First things first, mushrooms love the shade and cool environments. So, you'll want to find a spot that's shielded from direct sunlight—under a tree or beside a bush works great. The area should be well-draining too, so your mushroom bed doesn't become a swamp.

Preparing the Soil or Logs: If you're going for a soil bed, you'll want to clear the area of weeds and lay down some cardboard as a base to prevent them from coming back. For log cultivation, choose hardwood logs like oak or maple, and make sure they're fresh—ideally cut within the last six weeks.

Inoculating with Mushroom Spawn: This is where the magic starts. You'll mix mushroom spawn into your soil or drill holes into your logs to insert the spawn. Think of spawn as the seedlings of the mushroom world. You can use grain or sawdust spawn, but sawdust is often recommended as it's less prone to contamination.

Layering Your Materials: For soil beds, create a lasagna-like layering of wood chips, straw, and spawn. The wood chips provide the carbon-rich material mushrooms feast on, while the straw retains moisture. For logs, after inserting the spawn, seal the holes with wax to keep out contaminants.

Nurturing Over Time: Mushrooms need moisture, so keep your bed damp but not soggy. A light misting regularly should do the trick. Covering the bed with straw or burlap can help retain moisture. For logs, stack them in a crisscross pattern in a shady spot and keep them moist.

Harvesting Your Mushrooms: Patience is key. It might take a few months before you see the fruits of your labor. When the mushrooms are plump and the edges are still curled down, they're ready to harvest. Just twist them gently at the base, and voilà!

Practical Tips:

- Wine Cap mushrooms are great for beginners and can grow as big as dinner plates!
- Keep an eye out for pests and manage them by maintaining a clean bed.
- Add fresh wood chips annually to keep your soil bed productive.

Remember, every mushroom species has its own preferences, so tailor your approach to what you're growing. With a bit of care and attention, you'll have a flourishing mushroom garden that's both a joy to tend and to harvest.

Companion Planting and Permaculture

Let's dive into the symbiotic trio of companion planting, permaculture, and outdoor mushroom gardening.

Companion Planting: This is the practice of placing plants together that can help each other grow. For mushrooms, this means partnering them with plants that can provide shade and maintain soil moisture. Think of it like finding a good neighbor for your mushrooms; someone who shares the water without flooding your yard.

Permaculture Principles: These are all about working with nature, not against it. It's like setting up a self-sustaining village for your plants and fungi. By mimicking natural ecosystems, we create gardens that are more resilient and require less maintenance. For mushrooms, this means creating a space where they can thrive under the canopy of taller plants, just like they would in the forest.

Outdoor Mushroom Gardening: Mushrooms are the recyclers of the garden, breaking down organic matter and returning nutrients to the soil. They're like the garden's cleanup crew, working behind the scenes to keep everything running smoothly.

Practical Tips:

- **Start Small:** Begin with easy-to-grow mushroom species like oyster or shiitake.
- **Shade Lovers:** Plant leafy greens like spinach or chard nearby to provide gentle shade.
- **Wood Chips and Straw:** Use these as mulch to create a moist, hospitable environment for your fungi friends.
- **Water Wisely:** Mushrooms love moisture, but too much can be harmful. Water plants in a way that keeps the soil damp but not soggy.

Examples:

- **The Three Sisters and a Fungus:** Borrowing from the Native American tradition of planting corn, beans, and squash together, add mushrooms to the mix. The corn provides a stalk for beans to climb, the beans fix nitrogen in the soil, the squash

shades the ground, and the mushrooms
break down organic matter, enriching the
soil.

- **Herb Guardians:** Plant herbs like thyme
or parsley around your mushrooms. They'll
act as natural pest deterrents while adding to
the biodiversity of your garden.

CHAPTER FOUR

Harvesting and Storage

When and How to Harvest Mushrooms

Harvesting mushrooms can feel like a treasure hunt in your own backyard. It's a process filled with anticipation and delight, especially when you spot the signs that your fungal friends are ready to join you in the kitchen.

When are Mushrooms Ready to Harvest? Mushrooms are quite the silent communicators. They'll tell you they're ready through their **size**, **color**, and **texture**. Most varieties have a sweet spot in size, not too small that you'd miss them, and not too large that they've lost their tender charm. A mushroom in its prime often has a firm, yet slightly spongy feel, and its color should be vibrant, not faded or discolored.

How to Harvest Mushrooms The technique is simple but requires a gentle touch. For mushrooms like **shiitakes**, twist them off at the stem; it's like unscrewing a lightbulb. For **oyster mushrooms**, you'll want to cut them at the base with a knife. And for those delicate **chanterelles**, ease them out of the ground with a gentle pull.

Remember, mushrooms are like the apples of the forest; if you tug too hard, you might disturb their roots, which are planning the next batch of goodies.

A Personal Touch I remember the first time I harvested mushrooms. I was so worried I'd hurt them, but as I twisted my first shiitake free, it seemed to pop off with a satisfying 'thank you' for letting it fulfill its mushroom destiny. There's something magical about holding a mushroom you've grown yourself. It's a small, earthy connection to the world that fills you with a sense of accomplishment.

So, as you head out to harvest, think of it as a quiet conversation with nature. Be gentle, be patient, and most importantly, enjoy the moment. Your mushrooms are a gift, and they're ready to make your meals extraordinary.

Drying and Preserving Mushrooms

Harvesting Mushrooms for Optimal Freshness

Harvesting mushrooms at the right time is crucial for preserving their freshness and flavor. It's best to pick them just as the caps fully open and the gills are exposed. Use a sharp knife to cut the stem cleanly, which helps prevent damage to the mycelium and ensures future crops.

Drying Mushrooms for Long-Term Preservation

Drying is an effective way to preserve mushrooms, concentrating their flavor and allowing you to enjoy them for months to come. Here's how to do it:

Air Drying

- **Suitable for:** Most mushroom varieties, especially thin-fleshed ones like shiitake or oyster mushrooms.
- **Method:** Clean the mushrooms and slice them thinly. Spread them out on a wire rack in a well-ventilated, dry area away from

direct sunlight. A fan can speed up the
process.

- **Time:** 3-6 days, depending on humidity levels.

Oven Drying

- **Suitable for:** Thicker mushrooms like portobello.
- **Method:** Preheat your oven to the lowest setting (around 150°F or 65°C). Place sliced mushrooms on a baking sheet lined with parchment paper. Keep the oven door slightly open to allow moisture to escape.
- **Time:** 1-2 hours, checking periodically.

Dehydrator Drying

- **Suitable for:** All varieties, best for consistent and controlled drying.
- **Method:** Arrange sliced mushrooms on dehydrator trays. Set the temperature to 135°F (57°C) and let them dry until brittle.
- **Time:** 4-8 hours, depending on the mushroom type and thickness.

Practical Tips and Troubleshooting

- **Consistency:** Ensure slices are uniform for even drying.

- **Storage:** Once dried, store mushrooms in an airtight container in a cool, dark place.
- **Rehydration:** To use, soak dried mushrooms in warm water for 20-30 minutes.
- **Troubleshooting:** If mushrooms aren't drying evenly, rotate the trays or flip the slices halfway through the drying process.

Remember, the key to successful drying is low heat and good air circulation. With these techniques, you can savor the taste of your homegrown mushrooms long after the harvest season has passed.

Preserving Dried Mushrooms: Methods and Best Practices

Once you've successfully dried your mushrooms, preserving them properly is the next critical step to ensure they remain flavorful and safe for consumption. Here are some common preservation methods:

Vacuum-Sealing

- **Benefits:** Vacuum-sealing removes air, preventing oxidation and extending shelf life. It's ideal for long-term storage.
- **Limitations:** Requires a vacuum-sealer, which is an additional expense.
- **Best For:** Large quantities or if you have limited storage space.

Freezing

- **Benefits:** Freezing is convenient and effective for preserving the texture and flavor of mushrooms.
- **Limitations:** Freezer burn can occur if not sealed properly. Also, frequent power outages can compromise the preservation.
- **Best For:** Quick freezing and thawing, and for those with reliable electricity and freezer space.

Airtight Containers

- **Benefits:** Easy to use and doesn't require special equipment. Glass jars or food-grade plastic containers with tight-fitting lids work well.

- **Limitations:** Containers must be completely dry to avoid mold. Not as space-efficient as vacuum-sealed bags.
- **Best For:** Everyday use and for those who regularly consume dried mushrooms.

Labeling and Organizing

Labeling each container with the date of preservation and the type of mushroom is essential. This practice helps you keep track of freshness and ensures you use the oldest stock first. Organizing your preserved mushrooms in a cool, dark place like a pantry or cupboard will help maintain their quality. Avoid areas with temperature fluctuations or high humidity.

Optimal Shelf Life

Each preservation method has its own optimal shelf life:

- **Vacuum-Sealed:** Up to 1 year or more if kept in a cool, dark place.
- **Frozen:** 6-8 months, though some varieties may last longer.
- **Airtight Containers:** 6 months to 1 year, depending on the dryness and storage conditions.

By choosing the right preservation method for your needs and following these guidelines, you can enjoy your homegrown mushrooms' rich flavors all year round.8

Imagine you're walking through a forest, and there, peeking out from the underbrush, you find a cluster of wild mushrooms. It's like uncovering hidden treasure. You carefully harvest them, thinking of all the delicious dishes they'll inspire. But first, you'll need to preserve them, and that's where the real magic happens.

Drying mushrooms isn't just about preservation; it's an art form. Each slice you lay out to dry carries the promise of future culinary adventures. It's like sending a message to your future self, saying, "Here's a little burst of flavor, just when you need it."

And let's talk about **vacuum-sealing**—it's like putting your mushrooms into a time capsule. Every time you break that seal, it's a throwback to the day you harvested them, fresh and full of flavor.

Freezing might seem modern, but it's just another way of holding onto the essence of nature. It's like capturing a moment—the mushrooms' texture and taste paused in time, ready to spring back to life in your kitchen.

Using **airtight containers** is like building a library of flavors on your shelf. Each jar is a volume in the encyclopedia of your foraging and preserving efforts. And when you label them, it's not just practical; it's the title on the spine of each book in your collection.

Remember, there's no one-size-fits-all method here. Your kitchen, your rules. Maybe you'll find that a combination of techniques works best for you, or perhaps you'll invent a whole new method that we'll all be writing about someday.

So go ahead, **experiment**. Try different thicknesses when slicing, play around with drying temperatures, mix and match storage methods. Make mistakes—because that's how you'll learn and become the mushroom-preserving maestro you're destined to be.

And when you're done, sit back and marvel at your work. There's a certain pride that comes with preserving your own food. It's a connection to the earth and to the generations before us who made the most of nature's bounty. You're part of that tradition now.

So, here's to you, the beginner, the expert, the curious and the bold. May your mushrooms be many, and your pantry full of well-preserved, homegrown delights.

Troubleshooting Common Issues

Identifying Contamination

Identifying Contamination in Mushroom Cultivation: A Beginner's Guide

When you're starting out in the world of mushroom cultivation, it's like being a new gardener in an enchanted forest. Just as a gardener learns to spot the telltale signs of pests or disease in their plants, you'll need to become familiar with the signs of contamination in your mushroom crops. Here's a simple guide to help you on your journey.

Common Signs of Contamination

Off-Colors: Healthy mycelium, the vegetative part of a fungus, usually appears white and thread-like. If you notice colors like **green, yellow, or black**, think of them as unwelcome weeds in your mushroom garden. These colors often indicate mold or bacterial growth.

Strange Odors: A fresh mushroom culture should smell earthy and wholesome, like a forest after rain. If your nose wrinkles at a sour or musty scent, it's like stumbling upon a hidden bog—it's a sign that something's amiss.

Unusual Growth Patterns: Imagine your mycelium as a miniature city, with roads and buildings made of white threads. If you see structures that look more like tangled brambles than neat urban planning, you might be dealing with contamination.

Distinguishing Between Healthy and Contaminated Growth

Texture: Healthy mycelium feels like a firm spider web or a well-knit sweater. Contaminated areas might be slimy or sticky, similar to stepping on a slug in the garden.

Speed: Contaminants often race ahead of your mushroom mycelium. If you see rapid growth that's outpacing the rest of your culture, it's like weeds trying to overtake your garden plants.

Resilience: Give a gentle poke to your mycelium. Healthy mycelium bounces back, much like a well-watered plant. If it collapses or disintegrates, it's a sign of poor health.

Personal Anecdotes to Reassure You

Remember, encountering contamination is as normal as a gardener finding aphids on their roses. I once had a batch of oyster mushrooms that I was sure would be the envy of any cultivator. But one day, I noticed a patch of green mold, like a tiny invader in my mushroom kingdom. It was disheartening, but it taught me to be more vigilant, just as a gardener learns to spot the early signs of trouble.

Empowering Your Cultivation Journey

Trust your instincts. If something looks or smells off, it probably is. Don't be afraid to remove a contaminated section; think of it as pruning a rose bush to encourage healthy growth. Keep your cultivation area clean, like a chef keeps their kitchen, and always sterilize your tools, as a surgeon would before an operation.

By staying observant and proactive, you'll not only become adept at spotting contamination, but you'll also foster a resilient and thriving mushroom garden. Remember, every great cultivator started as a beginner, and every mistake is a stepping stone to success. Embrace the journey with confidence and curiosity, and watch as your mushroom crops flourish.

Pest and Disease Management

Ah, mushrooms! These delightful delicacies that sprout from the earth are not just a treat for our taste buds but also a joy for those who cultivate them. However, just like any other crop, mushrooms face their share of pesky intruders and ailments. Fear not, dear grower, for with a bit of know-how and vigilance, you can protect your fungal friends.

The Watchful Eye: Prevention is Key

First things first, keeping an eagle eye on your mushroom crop is paramount. Pests and diseases can be sneaky, but they leave clues. Regularly inspect your mushrooms for any signs of trouble, such as discolored spots, unexpected textures, or uninvited guests like mites or flies. Catching these early can mean the difference between a bountiful harvest and a fungal flop.

Organic Arsenal: Nature's Defenders

When it comes to defense, Mother Nature's got your back. Maintaining **proper humidity levels** is crucial; mushrooms love moisture, but too much can invite mold and bacteria. Strike a balance to keep them happy. Ensure **good air circulation** in your growing area to ward off stagnant conditions that pests adore.

Now, let's talk about some natural allies. **Neem oil** is a fantastic organic option that can deter a variety of pests without harming your mushrooms or the environment. And then there are the beneficial insects – think of them as the guardians of your garden. Ladybugs and predatory mites can help keep the pest population in check.

Tales from the Trenches: Grower's Triumphs

Let me share a little story. There was once a grower named Alex, who noticed tiny flies buzzing around her Shiitake mushrooms. Instead of panicking, Alex introduced a troop of ladybugs. Lo and behold, the ladybugs feasted on the flies, and the mushrooms thrived. It's these small victories that make the journey so rewarding.

Empowerment Through Education: You've Got This!

Remember, every grower faces challenges, but it's how you respond that defines your cultivation journey. Arm yourself with knowledge, and don't be afraid to try organic methods. With each obstacle Ah, mushrooms! These delightful delicacies that sprout from the earth are not just a treat for our taste buds but also a joy for those who cultivate them. However, just like any other crop, mushrooms face their share of pesky intruders and ailments. Fear not, dear grower, for with a bit of know-how and vigilance, you can protect your fungal friends.

The Watchful Eye: Prevention is Key

First things first, keeping an eagle eye on your mushroom crop is paramount. Pests and diseases can be sneaky, but they leave clues. Regularly inspect your mushrooms for any signs of trouble, such as discolored spots, unexpected textures, or uninvited guests like mites or flies. Catching these early can mean the difference between a bountiful harvest and a fungal flop.

Organic Arsenal: Nature's Defenders

When it comes to defense, Mother Nature's got your back. Maintaining proper humidity levels is crucial; mushrooms love moisture, but too much can invite mold and bacteria. Strike a balance to keep them happy. Ensure good air circulation in your growing area to ward off stagnant conditions that pests adore.

Now, let's talk about some natural allies. Neem oil is a fantastic organic option that can deter a variety of pests without harming your mushrooms or the environment. And then there are the beneficial insects – think of them as the guardians of your garden. Ladybugs and predatory mites can help keep the pest population in check.

Tales from the Trenches: Grower's Triumphs

Let me share a little story. There was once a grower named Alex, who noticed tiny flies buzzing around her Shiitake mushrooms. Instead of panicking, Alex introduced a troop of ladybugs. Lo and behold, the ladybugs feasted on the flies, and the mushrooms thrived. It's these small victories that make the journey so rewarding.

Empowerment Through Education: You've Got This!

Remember, every grower faces challenges, but it's how you respond that defines your cultivation journey. Arm yourself with knowledge, and don't be afraid to try organic methods. With each obstacle you overcome, you'll not only grow mushrooms but also confidence and resilience.

So, gather your neem oil, rally your insect allies, and march forth into your mushroom field with the assurance that you are fully equipped to tackle any challenge that comes your way.you overcome, you'll not only grow mushrooms but also confidence and resilience.

So, gather your neem oil, rally your insect allies, and march forth into your mushroom field with the assurance that you are fully equipped to tackle any challenge that comes your way.

Solving Environmental Challenges

Have you ever considered that the humble mushroom under your feet could be a superhero in disguise? It's true! Mushrooms are not just for pizzas and potions; they are powerful allies in our quest to heal the Earth. Let's delve into the fascinating world of mushroom cultivation and discover how these remarkable organisms can help us tackle some of the most pressing environmental challenges.

Soil Regeneration: The Mycelium Network's Magic Mushrooms start their life as mycelium, a network of tiny threads that work like nature's internet, connecting plants and trees. But their role doesn't stop at communication. They are also master decomposers, breaking down organic matter and returning nutrients to the soil. This process is vital for **soil regeneration**, especially in areas ravaged by pollution or deforestation. For example, the oyster mushroom has been used to break down petroleum products in contaminated soils, effectively **cleaning up oil spills** without the use of harmful chemicals.

Water Purification: Filtration Powerhouses
Mushrooms can also purify water. Their mycelium acts like a natural filter, trapping and breaking down pollutants. In one inspiring case, a community in Mexico used fungi to reduce lead contamination in their water supply. By introducing mushroom spores into the water, they saw a significant decrease in lead levels, making their water safer to drink.

Waste Management: Turning Trash into Treasure When it comes to waste management, mushrooms are the ultimate recyclers. They can transform agricultural waste, like straw or sawdust, into rich compost. Even more impressive, certain species can digest plastics, offering a glimmer of hope in our fight against plastic pollution.

How You Can Make a Difference Now, you might be wondering, "How can I join this environmental revolution?" It's simpler than you think! Here's how you can start:

1. **Educate Yourself**: Learn about different mushroom species and their environmental benefits.
2. **Start Small**: Grow mushrooms at home using a kit. It's a fun and educational activity for the whole family.

3. **Spread the Word**: Share your mushroom cultivation journey with friends and community members.
4. **Think Big**: Collaborate with local environmental groups to initiate larger mushroom remediation projects.

CHAPTER FIVE

Exploring Gourmet and Medicinal Varieties

Popular Gourmet Mushrooms

Step into the world of gourmet mushrooms, where each cap and stem holds a treasure trove of healing properties. In this section, we'll meander through the medicinal mushroom garden, uncovering the secrets of **Reishi**, **Lion's Mane**, and **Turkey Tail**—the triumvirate of wellness.

Reishi: The Mushroom of Immortality

First, let's get acquainted with Reishi, also known as **Ganoderma lucidum**. Revered in Eastern medicine as the "Mushroom of Immortality," Reishi has a **woody texture** and a **bitter taste**, often used in teas or extracts rather than culinary dishes. Its claim to fame? Boosting the immune system. I've heard stories of people feeling more **vigorous** and **balanced** after introducing Reishi into their routine. It's like finding an ancient wellspring of vitality.

Cultivating Reishi can be a meditative practice. They prefer **hardwood logs** or **sterilized sawdust**, and while they take their time to grow, the wait is a lesson in patience and the reward, a boost in well-being.

Lion's Mane: The Cognitive Culinary Delight

Next, we have the Lion's Mane, a mushroom that's as good for the brain as it is for the taste buds. With a flavor reminiscent of **seafood**, it's a fantastic meat substitute. But beyond its culinary uses, Lion's Mane is celebrated for its potential to **support nerve growth** and **cognitive function**. Imagine savoring a dish that not only pleases your palate but also nurtures your neurons.

For those looking to grow Lion's Mane, provide a **wood-based substrate** and maintain **high humidity**. It's a mushroom that rewards the attentive cultivator with both its beauty and its brain-boosting bounty.

Turkey Tail: The Canvas of Healing

Lastly, let's explore the Turkey Tail mushroom, named for its **colorful, fan-like appearance**. It doesn't have much of a flavor, which makes it perfect for teas and broths. Packed with

polysaccharides, Turkey Tail is a warrior in the fight against illness, supporting the immune system and offering hope to many.

Growing Turkey Tail is an exercise in sustainability, as it can help decompose wood while it grows. It's a reminder that in the cycle of life, there's a place for regeneration and healing.

Your Mushroom Wellness Journey

As you delve into the world of medicinal mushrooms, remember that they're more than just a food source—they're a **gateway to natural health**. Start with a simple tea or tincture, and as you become more confident, incorporate them into soups and stews. Each mushroom offers a unique gift of healing, waiting to be unwrapped by the curious and the health-conscious.

So, dear reader, I encourage you to open your heart and your kitchen to the therapeutic wonders of gourmet mushrooms. May your journey be filled with flavorful discoveries and wholesome healing.

Medicinal Mushrooms and Their Uses

Embark on an exploration of the marvelous world of medicinal mushrooms, where ancient wisdom meets modern wellness. These natural wonders, such as **Reishi**, **Chaga**, and **Lion's Mane**, are not only intriguing to learn about but also offer a plethora of health benefits that cater to both body and mind.

Reishi: The Sovereign of Serenity

Reishi mushrooms, often called the **"Sovereign of Serenity"** for their stress-relieving properties, are a cornerstone in the medicinal mushroom domain. With a history of use that spans millennia, Reishi is renowned for its ability to **enhance immune function** and **promote longevity**. Its woody texture and bitter profile lend themselves well to teas and soups, providing a grounding, earthy base that calms the spirit.

A friend once shared with me how adding Reishi tea to her evening routine helped her find a sense of calm after hectic days. It's anecdotes like these that highlight the personal touch these mushrooms can bring to our lives.

Chaga: The Diamond of the Forest

Chaga, the **"Diamond of the Forest,"** is a true gem when it comes to antioxidants. This mushroom grows on birch trees, resembling a charred lump of wood rather than a traditional mushroom. But don't let appearances deceive you; Chaga is a powerhouse, known to **support the immune system** and **fight inflammation**. It's commonly consumed as a tea, offering a subtle, vanilla-like flavor that warms the body and soul.

I recall a story of a mountaineer who swore by Chaga tea to rejuvenate his energy and protect his skin against the harsh mountain climate. It's amazing how nature provides us with such potent allies.

Lion's Mane: The Mind's Ally

Lion's Mane mushroom is not just a culinary delight with its seafood-like taste; it's also a cognitive champion. Studies suggest that Lion's Mane can **support brain health, enhance focus**, and even **aid in nerve regeneration.**

Whether it's stirred into a risotto or brewed into a tea, this mushroom is a testament to the saying, "Let food be thy medicine."

A student once told me how incorporating Lion's Mane supplements into her diet improved her concentration during exam season. It's stories like this that underscore the tangible benefits these fungi can offer.

Incorporating Medicinal Mushrooms into Your Life

Bringing medicinal mushrooms into your daily routine can be as simple as brewing a morning tea or adding a spoonful of mushroom powder to your smoothie. For the culinary adventurers, try adding finely chopped medicinal mushrooms to your dishes for an extra health kick. Remember, the key is consistency and enjoyment—find a way to make these mushrooms a part of your life that feels natural and sustainable.

So, dear reader, I invite you to open your mind and your pantry to the potential of medicinal mushrooms. May your journey be filled with healthful discoveries and a renewed sense of well-being. Here's to your health—naturally and deliciously!

Medicinal Mushrooms and Their Uses

As we delve into the enchanting world of gourmet and medicinal mushrooms, it's crucial to navigate the legal and ethical pathways that ensure our cultivation practices honor both the law and the earth. This section is dedicated to guiding beginners through the responsibilities that come with the role of a mushroom cultivator.

Legal Groundwork: Permits and Licenses

Before you plant your first spore, it's imperative to understand that certain mushroom species, especially those with psychoactive properties, are regulated under law. Compliance with local regulations is not optional; it's a cornerstone of responsible cultivation. Depending on your location, you may need to obtain permits or licenses that align with zoning, land use, and environmental protection. These legal steps are in place to safeguard both the cultivator and the community, ensuring that your mushroom venture is legitimate and safe.

Ethical Harvest: Sustainability and Conservation

The ethical compass of mushroom cultivation points towards sustainability and conservation. It's not just about what we take from the earth, but also what we give back. Sustainable practices such as using organic substrates, minimizing water waste, and ensuring proper disposal of spent materials are not just good habits—they're acts of respect for our planet.

Responsible foraging is another pillar of ethical mushroom exploration. It means taking only what you need, leaving enough for the ecosystem to regenerate, and ensuring that future generations can enjoy the same bounty. Remember, every mushroom picked is a part of a delicate ecological balance.

Sourcing with Integrity: Spawn and Spores

When it comes to sourcing mushroom spawn or spores, transparency and integrity should be your guiding principles. Opt for reputable suppliers who provide quality, uncontaminated products4. This not only guarantees the health of your mushrooms but also supports ethical businesses that prioritize sustainable practices.

Real-Life Impact: Anecdotes of Ethical Cultivation

Consider the story of a local farmer who, by sourcing spawn ethically and employing sustainable methods, transformed a small plot into a thriving mushroom haven. This farmer's commitment to legal and ethical practices not only yielded a bountiful harvest but also inspired the community to value the integrity of their food sources.

Cultivating with Compassion

As you embark on your mushroom cultivation journey, let compassion for the natural world be your constant companion. Approach each step with mindfulness, from legal compliance to ethical harvesting, and you'll find that the rewards extend far beyond the dinner plate. Your actions can contribute to a healthier planet and a more connected community, fostering a legacy of stewardship for the fascinating fungi kingdom.

In summary, cultivating gourmet and medicinal mushrooms is a journey that intertwines with the larger tapestry of our environment and society. By adhering to legal guidelines, embracing ethical practices, and sourcing responsibly, you become not just a cultivator of mushrooms but also a cultivator of good in the world.

Crafting Nature's Cure – The Medicinal Magic of Mushrooms

1. Reishi Mushroom Tea:
   - Ingredients: Dried reishi mushrooms, water
   - Measurements: 2-3 dried reishi slices per cup of water
   - Preparation: Boil water and add dried reishi slices. Simmer for 20-30 minutes. Strain and enjoy.
   - Benefits: Supports immune function, reduces stress, promotes relaxation

2. Turkey Tail Mushroom Tincture:
   - Ingredients: Dried turkey tail mushrooms, alcohol (e.g., vodka)
   - Measurements: 1 part dried turkey tail to 5 parts alcohol
   - Preparation: Place dried mushrooms in a glass jar and cover with alcohol. Seal and let steep for 4-6 weeks, shaking occasionally. Strain and store in a dark bottle.

- Benefits: Boosts immune system, supports digestion, may aid in cancer treatment

3. Lion's Mane Mushroom Soup:

- Ingredients: Fresh lion's mane mushrooms, vegetable broth, garlic, onions, olive oil
- Measurements: 200g of lion's mane mushrooms per serving
- Preparation: Sauté garlic and onions in olive oil. Add sliced lion's mane mushrooms and vegetable broth. Simmer for 20 minutes. Season to taste.
- Benefits: Improves cognitive function, supports nerve health, enhances digestion

4. Shiitake Mushroom Stir-Fry:

- Ingredients: Fresh shiitake mushrooms, soy sauce, sesame oil, vegetables (e.g., bell peppers, broccoli)
- Measurements: 150g of shiitake mushrooms per serving
- Preparation: Slice shiitake mushrooms and stir-fry with vegetables in sesame oil and soy sauce until tender.
- Benefits: Boosts immune system, supports heart health, may aid in weight loss

5. Chaga Mushroom Extract:

- Ingredients: Dried chaga mushrooms, water, honey (optional)
- Measurements: 2-3 tablespoons of dried chaga per cup of water
- Preparation: Simmer dried chaga in water for 4-6 hours. Strain and sweeten with honey if desired.
- Benefits: Rich in antioxidants, boosts energy, supports liver health

6. Maitake Mushroom Capsules:

- Ingredients: Dried maitake mushrooms, empty gel capsules
- Measurements: Fill each gel capsule with powdered dried maitake mushrooms
- Preparation: Grind dried maitake mushrooms into a fine powder. Fill gel capsules with the powder.
- Benefits: Regulates blood sugar, supports immune function, may aid in weight management

7. Oyster Mushroom Ointment:

- Ingredients: Fresh oyster mushrooms, coconut oil, beeswax
- Measurements: 200g of oyster mushrooms, 1 cup coconut oil, 2 tablespoons beeswax
- Preparation: Infuse coconut oil with sliced oyster mushrooms over low heat for 4-6 hours. Strain and add melted beeswax. Pour into jars and let cool.

- Benefits: Soothes skin irritation, promotes wound healing, reduces inflammation

8. Cordyceps Mushroom Smoothie:

- Ingredients: Fresh or powdered cordyceps mushrooms, banana, spinach, almond milk
- Measurements: 1 teaspoon of powdered cordyceps or 50g of fresh mushrooms per smoothie
- Preparation: Blend all ingredients until smooth.
- Benefits: Increases energy and endurance, improves respiratory function, supports kidney health

9. Enoki Mushroom Salad:

- Ingredients: Fresh enoki mushrooms, mixed greens, cherry tomatoes, balsamic vinaigrette
- Measurements: 100g of enoki mushrooms per serving
- Preparation: Rinse and trim enoki mushrooms. Toss with mixed greens, cherry tomatoes, and balsamic vinaigrette.
- Benefits: Supports immune system, aids in digestion, promotes healthy skin

10. Porcini Mushroom Risotto:

- Ingredients: Dried porcini mushrooms, Arborio rice, vegetable broth, Parmesan cheese, garlic, onion

- Measurements: 50g of dried porcini mushrooms
per serving
   - Preparation: Soak dried porcini mushrooms in
warm water for 30 minutes. Sauté garlic and onions
in olive oil. Add Arborio rice and stir in vegetable
broth gradually until cooked. Stir in soaked porcini
mushrooms and Parmesan cheese.
   - Benefits: Rich in antioxidants, supports brain
health, aids in digestion

11. Button Mushroom Pasta:
   - Ingredients: Fresh button mushrooms, pasta,
garlic, olive oil, parsley
   - Measurements: 200g of button mushrooms per
serving
   - Preparation: Slice button mushrooms and sauté
with garlic in olive oil until golden brown. Toss with
cooked pasta and chopped parsley.
   - Benefits: Supports immune function, aids in
weight management, promotes heart health

12. Shimeji Mushroom Miso Soup:
   - Ingredients: Fresh shimeji mushrooms, miso
paste, tofu, green onions, dashi broth
   - Measurements: 150g of shimeji mushrooms per
serving
   - Preparation: Sauté shimeji mushrooms in dashi
broth. Add cubed tofu and miso paste. Simmer until

heated through. Garnish with chopped green
onions.
   - Benefits: Supports digestive health, boosts
immune system, rich in probiotics

13. Wood Ear Mushroom Stir-Fry:
   - Ingredients: Fresh wood ear mushrooms, garlic,
ginger, soy sauce, sesame oil
   - Measurements: 100g of wood ear mushrooms
per serving
   - Preparation: Slice wood ear mushrooms and
stir-fry with garlic and ginger in sesame oil and soy
sauce until tender.
   - Benefits: Supports cardiovascular health, aids in
blood circulation, rich in iron

14. King Trumpet Mushroom Skewers:
   - Ingredients: Fresh king trumpet mushrooms,
bell peppers, onions, balsamic glaze
   - Measurements: 200g of king trumpet
mushrooms per serving
   - Preparation: Slice king trumpet mushrooms and
thread onto skewers with bell peppers and onions.
Grill until tender. Drizzle with balsamic glaze.
   - Benefits: Supports bone health, aids in weight
loss, promotes satiety

15. Mushroom Broth:

  - Ingredients: Assorted mushroom trimmings (e.g., stems, scraps), vegetable scraps (e.g., onion skins, carrot peels), water
  - Measurements: Fill a large pot with mushroom and vegetable scraps. Cover with water.
  - Preparation: Simmer scraps in water for 1-2 hours. Strain and use as a base for soups, stews, and sauces.
  - Benefits: Rich in nutrients, supports immune function, adds depth of flavor to dishes

Each of these mushroom medicines offers a unique way to incorporate mushrooms into one's diet and lifestyle, providing potential health benefits while also delighting the taste buds. Adjust ingredients and measurements according to personal preference and dietary needs.

CONCLUSION

As we close the final pages of our journey together, let us take a moment to reflect on the rich tapestry of lessons woven throughout our mushroom cultivation adventure. You've not only learned the **practical skills** necessary to nurture these fascinating fungi from spore to harvest, but you've also embraced the **thrill of discovery** and the **joy of growth**—both of your mushrooms and your own personal development.

Through this process, you've seen firsthand the virtues of **patience** and **curiosity**, and how they intertwine with the delicate threads of nature. You've experienced the wonder of life as it unfolds in the gills and caps of your mushroom crop, and understood that each mushroom is a testament to the care and attention you've invested.

Remember, every question you asked, every challenge you faced, was a step towards a deeper connection with the natural world. Your mistakes were not setbacks, but rather stepping stones to greater knowledge and skill. And every harvest, whether it filled a basket or just your hand, was a victory to be celebrated.

As you continue on your path, let the spores of wisdom you've collected germinate within you. Let them grow into a forest of possibilities, leading you to new horizons and new adventures in the world of mushrooms.

Thank you for allowing me to be a part of your story. Your journey does not end here; it is just beginning. May your love for mushrooms and the natural world flourish, and may you always find joy in the simple pleasure of watching life grow.

With heartfelt gratitude and warm wishes for your continued exploration,

Your Companion in Cultivation